# Extreme Experiments

**ANN O. SQUIRE**

**Children's Press®**
An Imprint of Scholastic Inc.
New York   Toronto   London   Auckland   Sydney
Mexico City   New Delhi   Hong Kong
Danbury, Connecticut

**Content Editor**
Robert Wolffe, EdD
Professor
Bradley University, Peoria, Illinois


Library of Congress Cataloging-in-Publication Data
Squire, Ann, author.
 Extreme experiments / by Ann O. Squire.
  pages cm. — (A true book)
 Audience: 9–12.
 Audience: Grade 4 to 6.
 Includes bibliographical references and index.
 ISBN 978-0-531-20742-0 (library binding : alk. paper) — ISBN 978-0-531-21553-1 (pbk. : alk. paper)
 1. Science—Experiments—Juvenile literature. I. Title.
 Q182.3.S68 2015
 507.8—dc23                                   2014005455

All rights reserved. Published in 2015 by Children's Press, an imprint of Scholastic Inc.
Printed in China 62
SCHOLASTIC, CHILDREN'S PRESS, A TRUE BOOK™, and associated logos are trademarks and/or registered trademarks of Scholastic Inc.

1 2 3 4 5 6 7 8 9 10 R 24 23 22 21 20 19 18 17 16 15

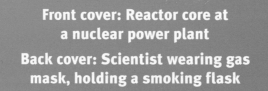

**Front cover: Reactor core at a nuclear power plant**
**Back cover: Scientist wearing gas mask, holding a smoking flask**

# Find the Truth!

**Everything** you are about to read is true *except* for one of the sentences on this page.

Which one is **TRUE**?

**T or F** Smallpox was one of the world's most deadly diseases.

**T or F** Experiments proved that a horse named Clever Hans could add, subtract, and spell.

Find the answers in this book.

# Contents

THE **BIG** TRUTH!

## Cloning a Sheep

**Dolly was the first successfully cloned sheep.**

**The Bikini Islands**

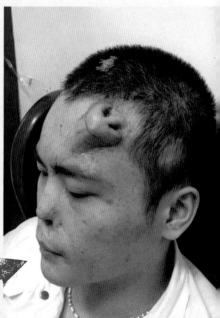

A surgeon first described using
forehead skin to replace an
amputated nose in 500 BCE.

5

A special suit was designed to protect an astronaut during a "walk" in space.

Decades of experiments have made it possible to survive in space.

# CHAPTER 1

# The Ins and Outs of Experiments

An experiment is a way of finding out about the universe. There are so many strange and wonderful things around us. Scientists often design equally strange experiments to learn about them. Think of catching a horse in a lie it didn't know it was telling. Or growing a new ear or nose for a patient to replace one that's been damaged. Some researchers have wiped out dangerous diseases. Others have turned entire islands deadly. No matter their design, experiments change the way we see the world.

# Designing an Experiment

An experiment is designed to answer a specific question. Experiments may be very simple or very complex. It depends on what sort of question the experiment is designed to answer. For example, a researcher might ask, "How does wearing a hat affect a person's temperature?" To answer this, the scientist makes a prediction. He or she then designs an experiment that will best test that prediction.

**Warmth is just one aspect of hats a scientist can study. A researcher might also study how different hats protect a head from rain or provide shade from the sun.**

The young man's hat is not the only variable in this picture. His coat, snow pants, and boots are other examples of variables.

# Testing a Hypothesis

Suppose our scientist predicts that a hat helps a person shiver less. This is called a **hypothesis**. The scientist might take this hypothesis one step further. He or she hypothesizes that the thicker a hat is, the less that person will shiver. To design an appropriate experiment, our scientist must deal with **variables**. Variables are things that could change. There are three kinds of variables: independent, dependent, and constant.

**Our researcher learns about how hats affect warmth by giving each subject a different hat to wear.**

# Variables

The independent variable is a change the scientist controls. He or she tells one person to wear a thick winter hat, another a ball cap, and a third no hat at all. The type of hat each person wears is the independent variable. The amount of shivering each subject experiences is the dependent variable. This variable changes, depending on the independent variable.

Constant variables should not change. The subject's clothing, his or her location, and the weather are examples of what can affect results. Imagine that the first subject wore a long-sleeved shirt and jeans. The other two wore shorts and T-shirts. The first subject shivers the least. Is this because he wore the warmest hat or because of his long sleeves and pants? To trust results, the scientist must keep constant variables the same for all subjects.

**Differences in what kind of weather the subjects experience affect an experiment's results.**

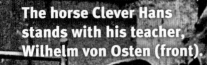

The horse Clever Hans stands with his teacher, Wilhelm von Osten (front).

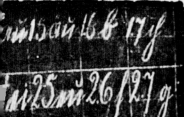

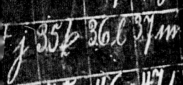

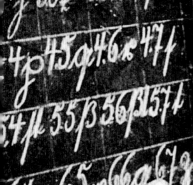

# CHAPTER 2

# Testing Animals

Scientists have long asked questions about animals. How much can they learn? How smart are they? A horse in Germany named Clever Hans was famous in the 1800s for his supposed intelligence. Hans could spell, tell time, and solve math problems. When asked a question, Hans tapped the answer with one of his front feet. If asked, "What is 2 plus 3?" Hans tapped his foot five times. People couldn't believe a horse could be so smart.

Hans was trained by a former schoolteacher.

# How Does He Do That?

In 1904, a group of researchers concluded that Hans's abilities were real. But this answer was not good enough for a scientist named Oskar Pfungst. Pfungst designed his own experiment. When Hans was kept away from his audience, he answered correctly. When people other than Hans's owner asked the questions, he answered correctly. But when he could not see the questioner or the questioner did not know the answer, Hans failed miserably. What was going on?

Clever Hans's mentor gives Hans a lesson.

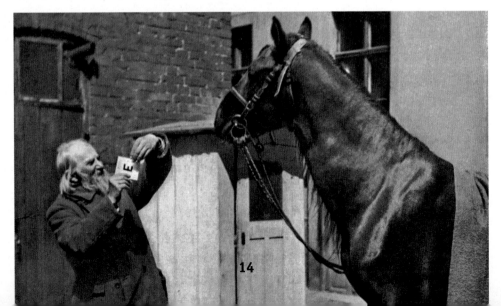

14

Hans was observant, but not necessarily intelligent.

## Subtle Cues

Pfungst found that Hans was responding to almost-invisible cues from his human partner. As Hans tapped an answer, he watched the person closely. When the horse reached the correct number of taps, the person would relax or change expression without realizing it. But Hans noticed this movement. He understood it as a signal to stop tapping. The horse was clueless if the questioner didn't know the answer or was out of sight.

**Vacanti's experiment provided a new method for replacing certain body parts.**

# A Mouse with Three Ears

Dr. Charles Vacanti wanted to help people who had injured or lost an ear. He figured out how to make cells from a cow grow into the shape of an ear. But the "ear" needed a blood supply to grow. Dr. Vacanti implanted the cells under a mouse's skin. The mouse's blood nourished the cells. The weird result was a mouse with what looked like a human ear growing out of its back!

# Fat Mice

Scientists also study animals to learn more about human problems. Obesity, or being very overweight, is a condition that affects many people. Mice can be obese, too. A type of mouse called "ob/ob" was known for its voracious appetite. Ob/ob mice ate constantly, getting fatter. As adults, ob/ob mice weighed three times as much as normal mice. Scientists wondered why these mice were always hungry, while normal mice knew when to stop eating.

**Scientists around the world have been studying different causes of obesity in mice to figure out ways to treat obesity in humans.**

Researchers made a small cut down one side of a normal mouse and one side of an ob/ob mouse. Then they sewed the two mice together so the mice shared the same bloodstream. Soon, the ob/ob mouse was losing weight. Researchers found that normal mice have the **hormone** leptin, which controls appetite, in their blood. Obese mice lack this hormone. When the ob/ob mouse shared a bloodstream with the normal mouse, it received the hormone and ate less. Scientists have found that leptin affects humans, too.

**Both of these mice are ob/ob mice. The mouse on the right has been given the hormone leptin.**

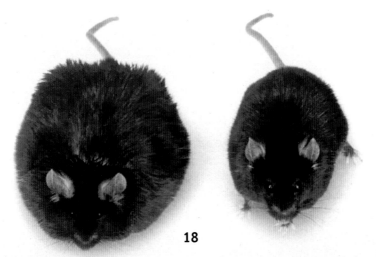

# Animal Experiments: Right or Wrong?

The results of animal experiments can be tremendously valuable to humans. But is it appropriate to do these experiments? Some people argue that experimenting on animals is a small price to pay for advances in human health. Others say it is unfair to inflict pain or discomfort on animals for any reason at all. People have been debating these questions for many years. Unfortunately, there are no easy answers. What's your opinion?

An astronaut floats outside the
International Space Station.

# CHAPTER 3

# Space, Time, and Curing the World

Can you imagine spending three months in bed? If so, you might qualify for the National Aeronautics and Space Administration's (NASA) bed rest study. It measures the effects of **microgravity** on the human body. This applies to astronauts spending long periods of time at the International Space Station 230 miles (370 kilometers) above Earth. It also helps experts plan future space missions.

A lab in space lets scientists study how space travel affects the human body.

# Living in Bed

Participants spend three months lying down. Their heads rest about 6 inches (15 centimeters) lower than their feet. Eating, sleeping, showering, and using the bathroom are all done in this position. Without exercise, a person's bones and muscles get weaker and fitness level decreases. This is similar to what happens in a weightless environment. Some research subjects do exercises while in bed. Scientists hope these experiments will show how to keep astronauts healthy in space.

**A test subject is helped out the door after spending 12 weeks in bed in NASA's bed rest study.**

Cosmonaut and scientist Boris Morukov ran the bed rest study in Moscow in the 1980s. He later flew missions with NASA.

# A Year in Bed

If you think three months in bed sounds boring, consider another experiment conducted in the 1980s. The test included 11 subjects in the Soviet Union, which is now Russia and surrounding countries. The volunteers spent 370 days in bed. The purpose of the experiment was the same as NASA's. It turned out that one of the biggest problems the subjects faced was boredom. Nevertheless, only one man quit the experiment before the year was up.

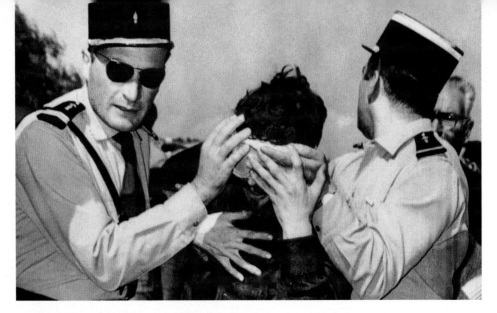

**Two police officers help Michel Siffre after his first cave experiment. Siffre had to cover his eyes to protect them from the light after being in the dark cave.**

# Life Underground

You might volunteer to spend a few months in bed. What about spending that time in a cave? This is what Michel Siffre did. In 1962, Siffre spent two months underground. He wanted to know how living without the sun or a clock would affect his understanding of time. His only access to the outside world was a phone line. He used this to report each time he woke up, ate, and went to sleep.

# Internal Time

Despite having no way to tell time, he still slept and woke on a cycle lasting just over 24 hours. He lost track of the days, though. When his team came to get him at the end of the experiment, he thought he still had a month to go. In later experiments, many other subjects developed a roughly 48-hour cycle. They were awake for 36 hours and then slept for 12 to 14 hours.

**Siffre took part in a second cave test in 1972. He spent 205 days in a cave in Texas.**

# The First Smallpox Vaccine

Would you test a **vaccine** for a deadly disease? Some experts estimate that smallpox has killed more people than all other infectious diseases combined. Smallpox causes fever, aches, and blisters that cover the body. Researchers had long looked for ways to prevent or cure smallpox. In the late 1700s, 13-year-old Edward Jenner heard that

people who caught the mild cowpox **virus** never caught smallpox. As a medical student years later, Jenner hypothesized that exposure to cowpox could prevent smallpox.

**Smallpox has affected people of all ages around the world.**

Nearly 200 years after Jenner's experiments, the world was officially declared free of smallpox.

## A Risky Test

Jenner first tested his prediction
in 1796. He chose the eight-year-old son of his
gardener as his subject. He infected the boy with
cowpox. The boy developed a blister and a fever, but
recovered. Then Jenner gave the child the smallpox
virus. To everyone's relief, he did not develop the
disease. Jenner's experiment led to the creation
of a smallpox vaccine. Vaccines have since been
developed for many diseases, including polio,
measles, and tetanus.

# Cloning a Sheep

In 1996, scientists in Scotland made history. They managed to clone a sheep, which they named Dolly. To do this, they used DNA. DNA is the blueprint for how an individual organism develops.

In normal reproduction, an organism gets DNA from both the mother and the father. The parents' DNA combines, mixing characteristics. For example, you may have gotten blue eyes from your father and left-handedness from your mother. You may be similar to both of your parents, but you are not exactly like either of them.

A clone is different. It is an exact copy of another organism. In Dolly's case, DNA was taken from a cell in her mother's body. This was inserted into an egg cell without any DNA from another sheep. Because she developed entirely from her mother's DNA, Dolly was an exact copy of her mother. In fact, she was her mother's identical twin!

Since then, mice, cows, pigs, deer, and other animals have been cloned. But as scientists learn more about the cloning process, there is concern that the technology could one day be applied to humans. Many people are afraid of what this could do to our species. What do you think?

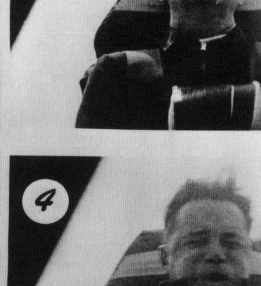

30

# CHAPTER 4

# Risky Endeavors

Some experiments can be incredibly dangerous. In the past, researchers at times chose to experiment on themselves instead of putting other subjects at risk. John Paul Stapp, a doctor and U.S. Air Force officer, was one of these researchers. He wanted to know if pilots could safely eject from planes traveling at the speed of sound. To test this, Stapp rode a "rocket sled." The sled reached superfast speeds before slamming to a stop.

During his experiments, Stapp used safety measures such as harnesses.

Experts estimate that seat belts saved almost 63,000 lives in the United States between 2008 and 2012.

## The Fastest Man Alive

On December 10, 1954, Stapp set a land speed record. He reached 632 miles (1,017 km) per hour in five seconds.

The accomplishment made him famous. He used his fame to push for better safety harnesses in military aircraft. He also argued for safety belts in cars. Thanks in part to Stapp, President Lyndon Johnson signed the Highway Safety Act in 1966. The law required seat belts in all new cars sold in the United States.

As a result of his high-speed experiments, Stapp suffered many injuries. He had concussions, or serious head injuries. He also suffered cracked ribs, broken bones, and permanent vision problems. He once explained, "I took my risks for information that will always be of benefit." Researchers search for ways to protect their subjects during such dangerous experiments. Experiments today are sometimes limited in the interest of safety.

**Technicians make last-minute adjustments to John Stapp and his rocket sled before a test.**

# Atomic Bomb Tests

One of the most dangerous experiments in human history took place on Bikini Islands. This is a group of beautiful tropical islands in the Pacific Ocean. The U.S. military tested the effects of **atomic weapons** on anchored ships there. Bikini Atoll was chosen because it was very isolated. There were 167 people living on the Bikini Islands at the time. They were moved to another island and told they could return after the tests were completed.

**Islanders move their belongings during the evacuation of Bikini Atoll in 1946.**

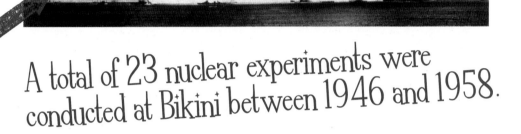

A total of 23 nuclear experiments were conducted at Bikini between 1946 and 1958.

On July 25, 1946, an atom bomb was detonated 90 feet (27 meters) beneath the ocean's surface. It sent a column of water 2,000 feet wide (610 m) into the sky. Many ships anchored for the test were destroyed. On the ocean floor, the blast created a crater more than 200 feet (61 m) deep. But the most serious damage was invisible. The bomb released a cloud of **radioactivity**. It contaminated the lagoon and everything in it.

**Bikinians discuss the fate of their islands.**

The Bikinian people were eager to return to their islands. However, radioactive contamination from the blasts was longer lasting than anyone had predicted. It was not until the 1970s that Bikinians were allowed to move back home. The United States continued to measure radiation levels. After several years, researchers found that radiation levels in the plants, animals, and well water were still dangerously high. Once again, the residents had to leave their islands.

# Bikini Atoll Today

The Bikini atomic tests have been widely criticized as overly dangerous and badly designed. If you visited Bikini Atoll today, you would see blue skies, white sand, sparkling clear water, and palm trees swaying in the breeze. But the soil of this tropical paradise is still contaminated with radioactive material. Plants that grow in the soil and animals that eat the plants all carry that radioactivity. The islands are still too dangerous for people to inhabit.

It will take some time, but doctors think Xie Wei will eventually regain the full use of his hand.

# CHAPTER 5

# Just Plain Weird

Some experiments are so strange that you have to see them to believe them. A Chinese factory worker named Xie Wei was operating a drilling machine when it accidentally cut off his right hand. The quick-thinking worker placed the hand in a bag of ice. He set out to look for a doctor who might be able to reattach it. After visiting several hospitals, he finally found one that could perform the delicate surgery.

Doctors reconnect blood vessels, nerves, muscle, and bone to reattach a severed limb.

## A Healthy Hand

However, Xie Wei's arm was badly injured. It needed time to heal before surgeons could reattach his hand. The doctors decided to temporarily attach the hand to Xie Wei's ankle. The ankle's blood supply would keep the hand alive until his arm healed. Xie Wei spent the next month as the only man in the world with a hand sticking out of his leg. Then doctors were able to reattach his hand to his arm.

# Timeline of Extreme Experiments

**1796**
Edward Jenner performs his first vaccination experiment.

**1904**
A team of researchers declares Clever Hans's abilities to be real.

**1946**
Researchers perform the first Bikini Atoll atomic test.

# A Nose on His Forehead

If you think the last experiment seems weird, consider the case of another Chinese man. He hurt his nose in a traffic accident. Doctors could not repair the nose. They decided to grow a new one—on the man's forehead! Though it looks extreme, the method is similar to other procedures that are used all the time. The doctors first placed expanders under the forehead's skin to create space for the new nose to grow.

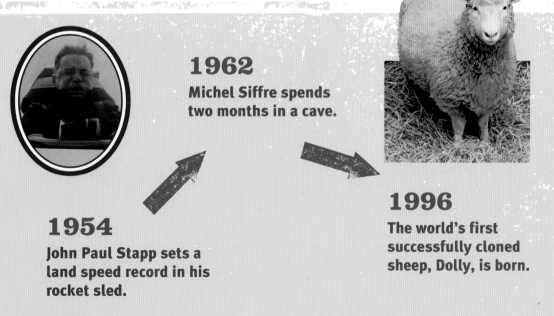

**1962**
Michel Siffre spends two months in a cave.

**1954**
John Paul Stapp sets a land speed record in his rocket sled.

**1996**
The world's first successfully cloned sheep, Dolly, is born.

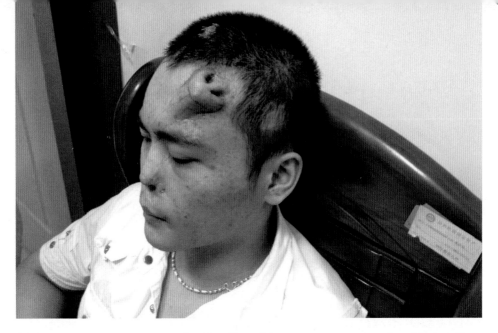

**The nose was grown on the forehead because a person's skin at the forehead is similar to the skin on the person's nose.**

Next, the man's doctors took cartilage from his ribs to fill in the nose. Cartilage is the tough, flexible tissue that gives a nose its shape. The blood supply in the man's forehead nourishes the new nose as it grows. When the nose is ready, the doctors will move it to the spot currently occupied by the damaged nose. A small scar on the man's forehead will be the only reminder of his strange experience.

# An Ear on Her Arm

In a similar case, a woman's cancer treatments badly damaged her ear. Doctors implanted cartilage from her ribs under the skin of her forearm. A new ear grew there for several months, and then was repositioned to the woman's head. She had some fun with the ear's unusual original location. When her children nagged her, she rolled up her sleeve and said, "Tell it to the arm!" Successes like this are what keep doctors and other researchers experimenting. ★

**Researchers are always experimenting with new ways to solve problems. What seems strange today may seem perfectly normal years from now!**

Number of U.S military and civilian personnel involved in the Bikini atomic experiments: More than 42,000

Number of people killed by smallpox during the 20th century: 300 million

Date of the last known natural case of smallpox: 1977

Estimated number of lives saved each year through the use of seat belts in automobiles: As many as 15,000

Percentage of adults in the United States who are obese: 35.7%

Estimated annual medical cost of obesity in the United States: $147 billion (2008 dollars)

## Did you find the truth?

(T) Smallpox was one of the world's most deadly diseases.

(F) Experiments proved that a horse named Clever Hans could add, subtract, and spell.

JANE MARBAIX

STERLING CHILDREN'S BOOKS

New York

# Acknowledgments.

The Zentangle® method was created by
Rick Roberts and Maria Thomas.

"Zentangle"®, the Zentangle logo, "Anything is possible
one stroke at a time", "Bijou", "Certified Zentangle Teacher", "CZT"®,
"Zentangle Apprentice"®, and "Zentomology" are trademarks, service marks,
or certification marks of Rick Roberts, Maria Thomas, and/or Zentangle Inc.

PERMISSION TO COPY ARTWORKS: The written instructions, designs,
patterns, and projects in this book are intended for the personal use of the
reader and may be reproduced for that purpose only. Any other use, especially
commercial use, is forbidden under law without the written permission
of the copyright holder.

All the tangles in this book are Zentangle originals created by Rick Roberts
and Maria Thomas, apart from: Barberpole by Suzanne McNeill
(blog.suzannemcneill.com); Heartrope by Bunny Wright, Canada; Cruffle by
Sandy Hunter, Texas, USA (tanglebucket.blogspot.co.uk).

The Zentangle Inspired Artwork on page 69 was created by June Bailey.

Dreamweaver stencils: http://www.woodware.co.uk

**STERLING CHILDREN'S BOOKS**
New York

An Imprint of Sterling Publishing
1166 Avenue of the Americas
New York, NY 10036

STERLING CHILDREN'S BOOKS and the distinctive
Sterling Children's Books logo are trademarks of
Sterling Publishing Co., Inc.

First Sterling edition published in 2015, under license from
Arcturus Publishing Limited
26/27 Bickels Yard, 151-153 Bermondsey Street,
London, UK, SE1 3HA

© 2015 by Arcturus Publishing Limited
Emily's Candy © Font Diner

Text, step-outs, and Zentangle Inspired Artworks:
Jane Marbaix (zentanglewithjane.me)
Design: Amy McSimpson and Tokiko Morishima
Project management: Frances Evans and Katie Woolley
Outline illustrations: Katy Jackson

ISBN 978-1-4549-1902-5

Distributed in Canada by Sterling Publishing
c/o Canadian Manda Group, 664 Annette Street
Toronto, Ontario, Canada M6S 2C8

For information about custom editions, special sales,
and premium and corporate purchases, please
contact Sterling Special Sales at 800-805-5489 or
specialsales@sterlingpublishing.com.

Manufactured in Canada
Lot #:
2 4 6 8 10 9 7 5 3
01/16

www.sterlingpublishing.com/kids

# Contents

# What is Zentangle?

Zentangle is a method of creating artwork by drawing simple tangles, or patterns, one line at a time. Zentangle isn't just about drawing. It focuses the mind, relaxes the body, and builds confidence. With Zentangle, "anything is possible, one stroke at a time."

## Why should I learn Zentangle?

Zentangle is great fun to do. The best bit is that anyone can do it! It has the happy knack of bringing out the artist in everyone, and this book will help you get started. Remember, the key thing is to take your time. Just go slowly and relax.

# What you need to get started!

## Pens and Pencils

You can begin making tangles with a pencil for drawing "strings" and for shading. Use a 01 (0.25 mm) black pen for fine lines, and a 08 (0.5 mm) black pen to fill in the darker areas of your pictures.

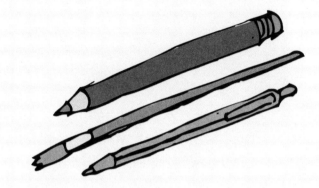

## Paper

Zentangle art is usually drawn on a square 3.5 inch (9 cm) tile. Good quality artist paper or white card is best to use, but you can use any kind of paper. It's a good idea to also have tracing paper on hand, so you can trace images to use as outlines.

## Extra Materials

Stencils are fun to use and can be found in art shops and online. Rubber stamps also make great outlines, but you'll need an inkpad to stamp them onto your paper. To brighten up your creations, you could use pens, pencils, or paints, too.

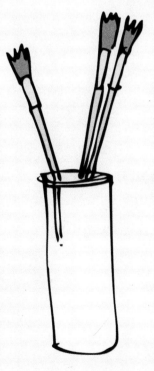

# What are "Strings?"

The Zentangle method is different from doodling as it begins with drawing "strings." These are pencil lines that separate spaces on your paper. The spaces are then filled with tangles. It's as simple as that!

All tangles have names and if you follow the steps, they are easy to do yourself.

A Zentangle is done on a 3.5 inch (9 cm) square tile. Larger pieces of art are called Zentangle Inspired Art (ZIA).

## How to draw strings

**1.** Pick up your pencil and draw a dot in each corner of your paper.

**2.** Join the dots to make a border.

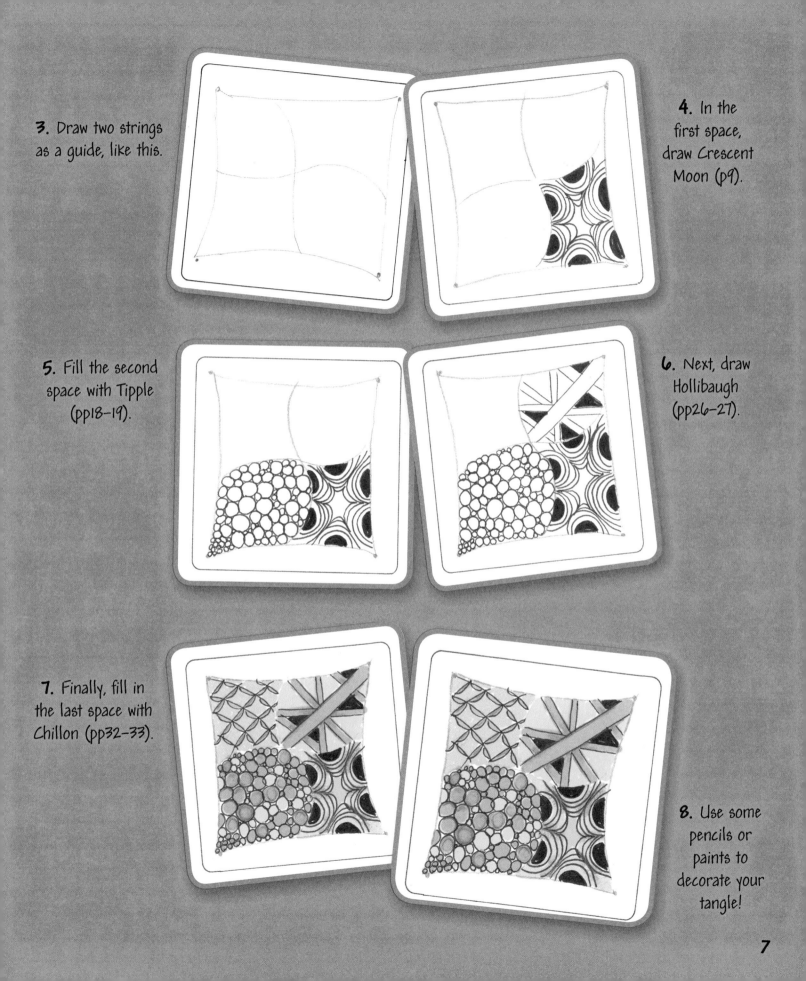

**3.** Draw two strings as a guide, like this.

**4.** In the first space, draw Crescent Moon (p9).

**5.** Fill the second space with Tipple (pp18–19).

**6.** Next, draw Hollibaugh (pp26–27).

**7.** Finally, fill in the last space with Chillon (pp32–33).

**8.** Use some pencils or paints to decorate your tangle!

# Getting Started

Now that you can create strings, let's begin by drawing some simple tangles. The pictures below show you how to draw Static, Crescent Moon, Msst, and Florz.

These tangles have been created by the Zentangle founders, Rick Roberts and Maria Thomas.

## Static

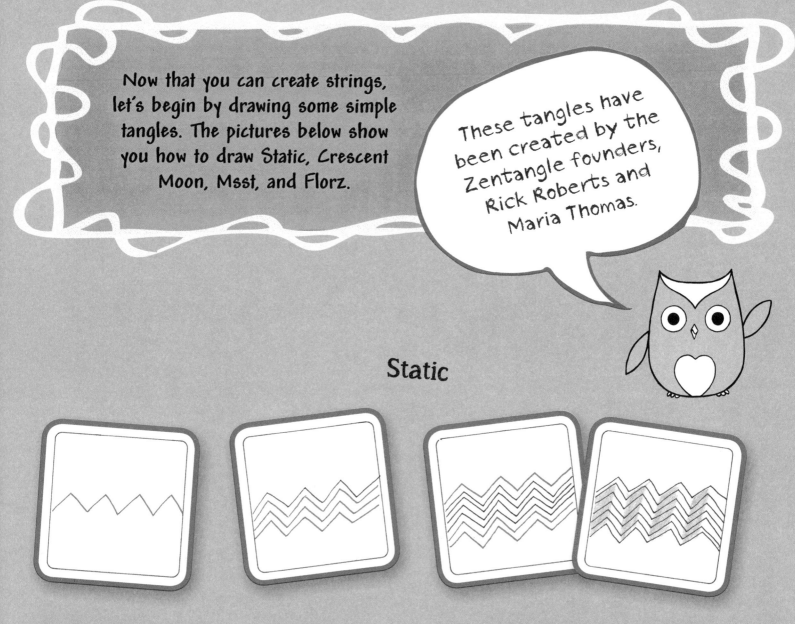

**1.** Draw a zigzag line from one side of your paper to the other.

**2.** Add some more zigzag lines below the first one.

**3.** Keeping adding zigzag lines to fill the space and some shading to finish it off.

# Crescent Moon

**1.** Draw semicircles around the edge of your paper and shade them in.

**2.** Draw a line around each shape.

**3.** Then, add another line around the shapes.

**4.** Finally, create a swirling cobweb pattern in the middle.

## Msst

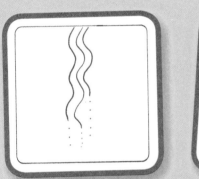

**1.** Draw three wavy lines from the top of your paper. Add three or four dots after each line.

**2.** Keep adding dots and lines to fill the space.

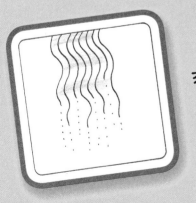

**3.** Shade your tangle to finish it off.

## Florz

**1.** Draw three lines from the top of your paper to the bottom. Then, draw three lines from one side to the other. This makes a grid.

**2.** Add a diamond shape to each crossing point on your grid.

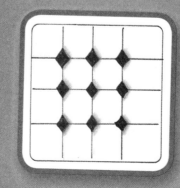

**3.** Finally, add some shade around the diamonds.

# How to Use this Book

Once you can draw some simple tangles, it's time to start experimenting. One way to do this is by creating Zentangle Inspired Artworks (ZIA). Throughout this book you'll find lots of great outlines of animals, flowers, and sea creatures that you can use to create your own ZIAs. Most of them already have strings drawn in. All you need to do is add some tantalizing tangles!

You can also buy stencils from craft shops to create ZIAs. Dreamweaver or Kala Dala stencils are really good to use.

**1.** Let's start with this fox outline. He's already got strings inside for his chest and the tip of his tail.

**2.** Draw a different tangle in each string. Pick something bold for his bushy tail.

Keeko
(pp34-35)

Paradox
(pp88-89)

Tipple
(pp18-19)

**3.** Choose some orange pencils or paints to finish off his beautiful coat. Your Zentangle Inspired Artwork is complete!

Zander
(pp40-41)

Crescent
Moon (p9)

You will often come across these words when you tangle:

**Shade**   This means using your pencil to darken areas of your tangle to make it POP.

**Highlight**   These are gaps in the lines you draw in your tangles. They can make your tangle SPARKLE.

**Aura**   If you trace around your tangle, you've added an aura. It can make your tangle come to life!

You can add tangles to us on every page, too!

# Knightsbridge

Knightsbridge is an easy tangle to try when you're getting started. It makes a simple grid pattern, which is perfect for this heart shape!

1. Draw diagonal lines from the top to the bottom of your paper. Then, draw lines from one side to the other. This makes a grid pattern.

2. Fill in every other square in your grid.

3. Finally, add some shade to your tangle.

You could even do straight grid lines, as I have in the heart shape on page 13.

I've used Knightsbridge to tangle this heart shape. Why don't you use Knightsbridge to tangle the heart below?

The following tangles have been used in this project:

KNIGHTSBRIDGE
'Nzeppel (pp90-91)

# Bales

Bales is great fun to draw, and it's simple, too! Follow these easy steps to make your own Bales tangle.

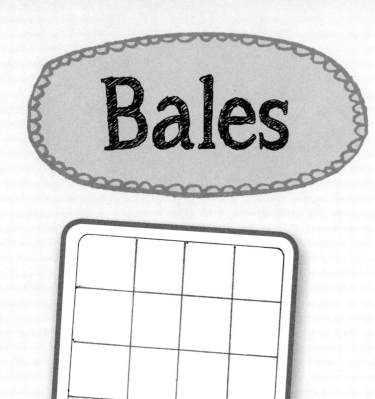

**1.** Begin by drawing a grid in your space.

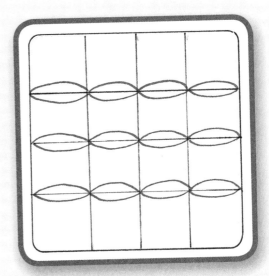

**2.** Add small oval shapes around the horizontal lines of each square in your grid.

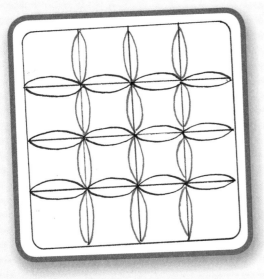

**3.** Then, do the same down the vertical lines.

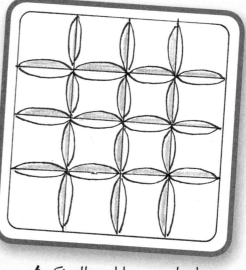

**4.** Finally, add some shade to your tangle.

Easy

You can use Bales and lots of other types of tangles to decorate this Kingfisher. I've tangled my own Kingfisher on the left!

The following tangles have been used in this project:

BALES
Poke Leaf (pp16-17)
Tipple (pp18-19)
Printemps (pp20-21)
Barberpole (pp28-29)
Keeko (pp34-35)
Meer (pp76-77)

Bales is one of the simplest tangles to do!

15

# Poke Leaf

Poke Leaf reminds me of the natural world all around. It's an ideal tangle to decorate this oak leaf shape.

**1.** Begin by drawing a stalk at the bottom of your paper. Then, draw a raindrop shape around the tip of the stalk.

**2.** Add more stalk and raindrop shapes to your paper.

**3.** Draw some shade onto your tangle.

**4.** Add an "aura" around each leaf for a different look. You can start this tangle anywhere on your paper, like I have done, and see where it takes you!

Poke Leaf fills this oak leaf perfectly. Can you copy the picture below to create your own leaf?

The following tangles have been used in this project:

POKE LEAF
Crescent Moon (p9)
Florz (p9)
Tipple (pp18-19)

Try different leaf shapes on your tangle to change the look!

# Tipple

Tipple is a great tangle to use for filling in bigger spaces in your creations. It creates a bubbly feel, which is perfect for this seahorse!

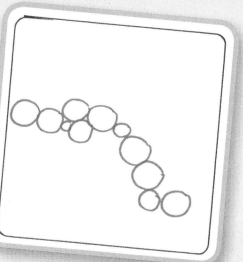

**1.** Begin by drawing a string of circles touching one another.

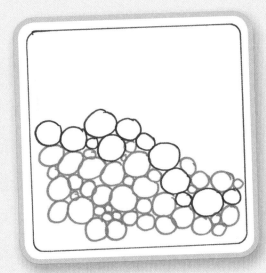

**2.** Draw more circles of different sizes to fill the space.

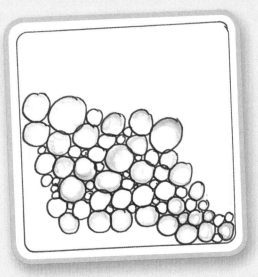

**3.** Finally, shade in the circles to give them more depth.

Tipple is one of the easiest tangles!

I have used Tipple along with some other tangles in the picture below. Why don't you try tangling the seahorse on the right?

Easy

The following tangles have been used in this project:

TIPPLE
Crescent Moon
(p9)
Poke Leaf
(pp16-17)
Printemps
(pp20-21)
Barberpole
(pp28-29)
Coral Seeds
(pp30-31)
Cubine
(pp70-71)

# Printemps

Printemps is a circular tangle that looks like lots of spirals joined together! It creates a busy tangle pattern. Why not give it a try?

1. Draw a small circle with a tiny gap, called a "highlight." Add more circles around this first one to make a spiral. You can draw a spiral without a highlight, too.

2. Create more spiral shapes to fill the space.

3. Finally, add a bit of shade to each spiral.

This is an ideal tangle to draw around a poem!

I have used Printemps and other tangles to brighten up this flower. Can you do the same?

The following tangles have been used in this project:

PRINTEMPS
Tipple (pp18-19)
Emingle (pp48-49)
Mooka (pp84-85)

# Bookmark

Bookmarks are useful to mark your place in the book you are reading and also make lovely gifts. Why not make your own, just like this one?

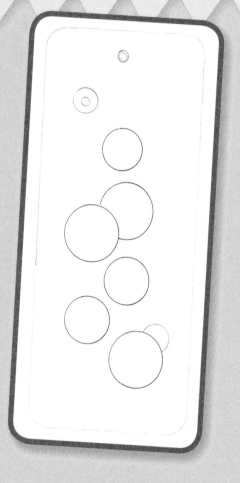

**1.** Cut out your bookmark from a piece of white paper. Then, draw some circles using a template (such as a pen lid) or a drawing compass.

**2.** Next, draw tangles in the circles and create funny animals, such as these birds. You can join the circles using Poke Leaf, too.

**3.** Add a black-and-white shade to your tangle for effect.

**4. Finally, mount your bookmark onto red card and add a dash of red to finish it off!**

The following tangles have been used in this project:

Crescent Moon (p9)
Poke Leaf (pp16-17)
Tipple (pp18-19)
Hollibaugh (pp26-27)
Barberpole (pp28-29)
Keeko (pp34-35)
Cruffle (pp42-43)
Gneiss (pp46-47)
Flux (pp82-83)

Why not create a double-sided bookmark by writing your name on the back and tangling it?

# Tangle Time!

Fill this starry night with your best tangles!

# Hollibaugh

Hollibaugh is a very relaxing tangle to do. You can draw straight or curvy lines, called "bands," or use a mixture of both. Just follow these simple steps!

1. Draw a "band" across your paper.

2. Each new band goes underneath the band it meets.

3. Add more bands to fill your space.

4. You can decorate the bands and background or leave them blank.

I have used Hollibaugh along with other tangles to fill my lion picture. Can you tangle your own lion on the right?

The following tangles have been used in this project:

HOLLIBAUGH
Crescent Moon (p9)
Tipple (pp18-19)
Printemps (pp20-21)
Barberpole (pp28-29)
Zander (pp40-41)
Flukes (pp56-57)
Paradox (pp88-89)
'Nzeppel (pp90-91)

This is probably the most well-known tangle of all!

27

# Barberpole

Barberpole is the perfect tangle for making borders or for running through your creations. Let's give it a try!

1. Draw a "band" across your paper.

2. Shade three short blocks inside the band, evenly spaced apart.

3. Draw two vertical lines on either side of each shaded block.

4. Your tangle is complete!

The following tangles have been used in this project:

BARBERPOLE
Crescent Moon (p9)
Florz (p9)
Tipple (pp18-19)
Printemps (pp20-21)
Hollibaugh (pp26-27)
Zander (pp40-41)

I've had great fun using Barberpole for this dog picture. Can you tangle the picture to create your own dog?

Can you use Barperpole to create a border around me?

29

# Coral Seeds

Coral Seeds is the perfect tangle for creating an underwater picture. That is why I have used it to fill this seashell.

1. Draw some wavy pairs of lines from the bottom left-hand corner of your paper.

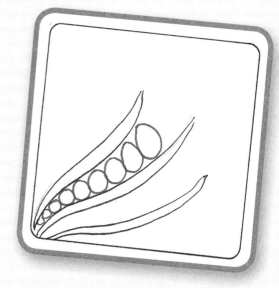

2. Then, fill in the blank spaces between the lines with circles.

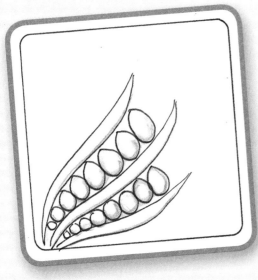

3. Add some shade to your tangle.

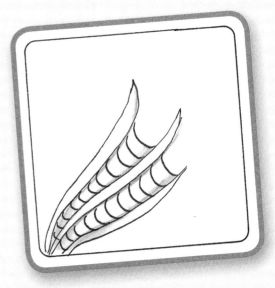

4. Change the look by filling the gaps with curved lines, like this.

The following tangles have been used in this project:

CORAL SEEDS
Finery (pp68-69)

This tangle is great for filling larger spaces in your drawings!

This shell has been created using Coral Seeds, along with another tangle. Why don't you try tangling your own seashell?

# Chillon

Chillon looks a little bit like Bales (pp14-15). It's easy to do when you follow these simple steps. Let's get started!

1. Draw a grid pattern on your paper.

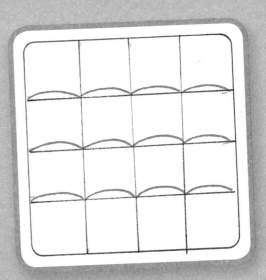

2. Add small half-moon shapes around the horizontal lines.

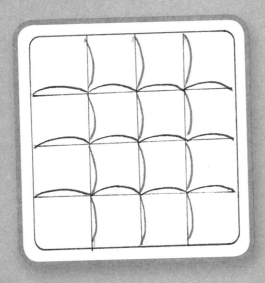

3. Then, draw more half-moon shapes along the vertical lines.

4. Don't forget to add some shade to your tangle.

You could change the size of your grid to create a different look.

The following tangles have been used in this project:

**CHILLON**
Crescent Moon (p9)
Poke Leaf (pp16–17)
Tipple (pp18–19)
Barberpole (pp28–29)
Cruffle (pp42–43)
Mooka (pp84–85)

Chillon creates a delicate feel so it's perfect for the wings of this butterfly. Why don't you use Chillon and other tangles to create your own butterfly?

# Keeko

This tangle looks a little bit like feathers, so it's great for this owl! Follow these steps to draw your own Keeko tangle.

1. Create a cross to begin. Draw three vertical lines in the top left square, then three horizontal lines in the top right square. Do the opposite in the squares below.

2. Repeat this pattern to create a band across your paper.

3. Add another row underneath.

4. Finally, shade your tangle to give it more depth.

Keeko makes lovely fur for animal projects!

The following tangles have been used in this project:

**KEEKO**
Tipple (pp18-19)
Yincut (pp60-61)
Cubine (pp70-71)
Flux (pp82-83)

You can use Keeko and other tangles to decorate your owl just like this one!

# Greeting Card

It's great fun making your own greeting cards. The special someone who you send the card to will also treasure it.

**1.** Use your pencil to draw a pattern onto a piece of paper. I have used a Kala Dala stencil here.

**2.** Add tangles to the stencil. I have used Mooka (pp84-85) for the hearts.

**3.** Fill your design with any tangles you like. I've used Tipple (pp18-19) for the inner petals.

**4.** I've also added circles and tangled them with Cruffle (pp42-43).

5. Finally, fold a piece of card in half and stick your design onto the front. Your beautiful card is ready to send!

The following tangles have been used in this project:

Tipple (pp18-19)
Cruffle (pp42-43)
Mooka (pp84-85)

You can also use letter stencils to trace someone's name, and then tangle the name to create a personalized greeting card!

# Tanglers' Gallery

Anyone can do it! Look at all this wonderful Zentangle Inspired Art.

Fish by Natalie Swanson, using a Dreamweaver stencil

Elephant, using a Dreamweaver stencil, and seahorse by Charlotte Taylor, age 8

Fish by June Bailey

Owl by Steffi Swanson, age 8,
using a Dreamweaver stencil

Racoon by Pippa Taylor,
age 6

Elephant by Anna Archer,
age 13

# Zander

Zander can be used in any creation. It's great for filling larger spaces, like this wolf's bushy tail!

1. Draw a "band" across your paper. Add pairs of loops around the band, 0.4 inch (1 cm) apart.

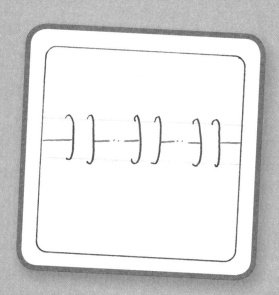

2. Next, draw a line through the middle of the band. Don't forget to lift your pencil every so often to add "highlights."

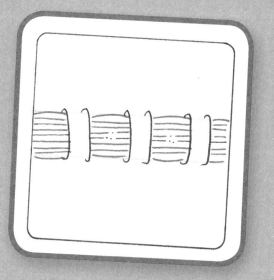

3. Add more lines within the band to fill the space.

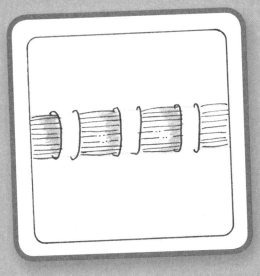

4. Finish by adding some shade to your tangle.

Try making the lines running through this tangle wavy for a different look.

The following tangles have been used in this project:

ZANDER
Crescent Moon (p9)
Tipple (pp18-19)
Hollibaugh (pp26-27)
Fracas (pp44-45)
Emingle (pp48-49)
Meer (pp76-77)

I have used Zander along with some other tangles in the picture on the right. Can you tangle your own wolf?

# Cruffle

I love to use Cruffle when making cards and bookmarks. Follow these simple steps to create your own Cruffle tangle.

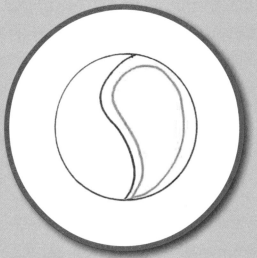

**1.** Start with a circle in the middle of your paper. Draw a wiggly line through the middle.

**2.** Draw a raindrop shape on the right-hand side, with the tip at the bottom of the circle.

**3.** Fill the right-hand side with raindrop shapes that get smaller and smaller.

**4.** Add some shade to your tangle.

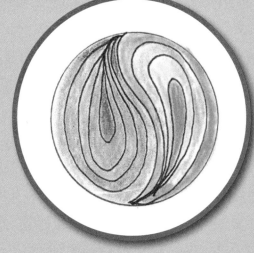

**5.** You can fill in the left-hand side, too, if you like.

Remember to take your time when tangling.

The following tangles have been used in this project:

CRUFFLE
Hibred (pp72-73)
Flux (pp82-83)

Cruffle makes a swirly tangle pattern, which is the perfect decoration for this cupcake. Why don't you give it a try?

# Fracas

Fracas uses crossing strokes, so it is ideal for filling in bigger spaces in your creations. Just follow these simple steps!

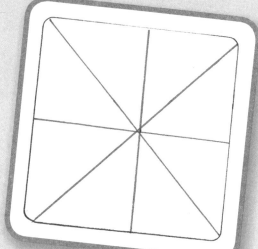

1. Draw four lines on your paper, making sure they cross through the middle.

2. Next, draw "auras" around your lines to create a star shape.

3. Start to fill in the spaces between the lines with wide horizontal strips.

4. Keep shading until your tangle looks like this.

44

I've used Fracas along with other tangles to fill this dolphin. Can you tangle your own dolphin?

The following tangles have been used in this project:

FRACAS
Tipple (pp18-19)
Coral Seeds (pp30-31)
Cruffle (pp42-43)
Paradox (pp88-89)

Try adding highlights to this tangle.

# Gneiss

This bold tangle is ideal for filling circular spaces. Just follow these simple steps to create the Gneiss tangle.

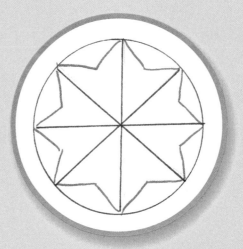

**1.** Draw a circle and add four lines inside it, making sure they cross in the middle, like the spokes of a wheel.

**2.** Next, add short, diagonal lines between the spokes, so that the shape looks like a star.

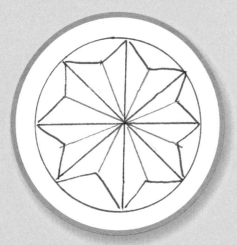

**3.** Draw some more lines from the middle of your star to meet the edge of your shape.

**4.** Shade in the left-hand side of each of the star's points.

Try changing the number of points on your star for a different look.

Gneiss creates a powerful feeling, which is perfect for this royal crown. Try tangling this crown below.

The following tangles have been used in this project:

**GNEISS**
Crescent Moon (p9)
Florz (p9)
Tipple (pp18-19)
Hollibaugh (pp26-27)
Emingle (pp48-49)
Flukes (pp56-57)

47

# Emingle

Emingle is made using a repeating pattern. It's great for filling large spaces! Follow these easy steps to draw your own Emingle tangle.

**1.** Create a grid, starting at the top left-hand corner of your paper.

**2.** Fill each square with a square spiral shape, starting at the same point in each one.

**3.** Repeat step 2 until all the spaces in your grid have been filled.

**4.** You can add some shade to each square for more depth.

Medium

I have created this elephant
picture using Emingle,
alongside other tangles.
Why don't you give it a try?

The following tangles have
been used in this project:

EMINGLE
Bales (pp14–15)
Poke Leaf (pp16–17)
Tipple (pp18–19)
Printemps (pp20–21)
Zander (pp40–41)
Man-O-Man (pp74–75)
Meer (pp76–77)

49

# Photo Frame

Follow these easy steps to make your very own Zentangle-inspired photo frame. Don't forget to add a photo!

**1.** Draw a frame onto a piece of white card, leaving enough space in the middle for your photo.

**2.** Make some strings within the frame. You could do straight lines or a more curved string.

**3.** Start to draw some tangles in the frame.

**4.** Then, add some shade to your tangles.

**5. Finally, place your photo in the middle of your frame using sticky tape or glue.**

The following tangles have been used in this project:

Static (p8)
Crescent Moon (p9)
Florz (p9)
Knightsbridge (pp12–13)
Bales (pp14–15)
Poke Leaf (pp16–17)
Tipple (pp18–19)
Printemps (pp20–21)
Hollibaugh (pp26–27)
Keeko (pp34–35)
Zander (pp40–41)
Cubine (pp70–71)
Flux (pp82–83)
Paradox (pp88–89)
'Nzeppel (pp90–91)

Don't forget to measure your photo so that your frame will fit around it.

# Tangle Time!

Bring this safari scene to life with tangles!

# Fife

Fife is a tangle that looks tricky, but it's actually quite easy to draw. All you need to do is follow these simple steps.

**1.** Draw four dots on your paper, evenly spaced to create a square shape.

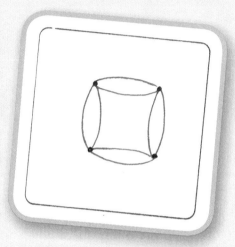

**2.** Add four oval shapes between the dots to create a rounded square.

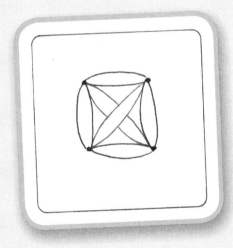

**3.** Draw an oval shape diagonally from the bottom right-hand corner to the top. Then draw another oval shape in the opposite diagonal direction, going underneath the shape you have just drawn.

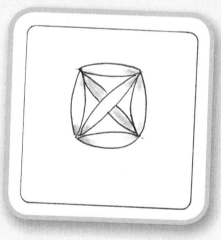

**4.** Add some shade to your tangle for more depth.

You can use Fife and lots of other tangles to decorate this cat. I have tangled my own feline friend here!

The following tangles have been used in this project:

**FIFE**
Tipple (pp18-19)
Zander (pp40-41)
Flux (pp82-83)
Mooka (pp84-85)

Remember to take your time with this tangle.

# Flukes

Flukes is an easy grid tangle to draw but looks very impressive when it's complete. Let's give it a try!

1. Create a grid, starting at the top left-hand corner of your paper.

2. Add "auras" inside a square. I have added four here. Then, shade in one corner of each square.

3. Fill all the squares on your paper with this pattern.

4. Finally, add some shade to your tangle.

Remember, an "aura" is an outline in or around your tangle.

The following tangles have been used in this project:

**FLUKES**
Crescent Moon (p9)
Tipple (pp18-19)
Flux (pp82-83)
Mooka (pp84-85)
'Nzeppel (pp90-91)

Flukes fills this boot perfectly. Take inspiration from the picture on the right to create your own boot!

# Jonqal

Jonqal is a fun, stripy tangle to draw. It can look very bold and stand out in the middle of your art, so it is perfect for this bear!

**1.** Draw two diagonal bands across your paper, like this.

**2.** Add zigzag lines across the bands, evenly spaced.

**3.** Shade in every other rectangle space.

**4.** You can add shade to some of the other spaces, too, or leave them white.

I have used this 3-D tangle in my picture to create a big, bold bear! Can you tangle your own bear?

The following tangles have been used in this project:

JONQAL
Crescent Moon (p9)
Knightsbridge (pp12–13)
Tipple (pp18–19)
Cubine (pp70–71)
Flux (pp82–83)

The shading is what makes this tangle look great!

# Yincut

Yincut can be quite a tricky tangle to draw, so remember to take your time. The more shade you add, the more 3-D it looks!

1. Start by drawing a simple grid to fill your paper.

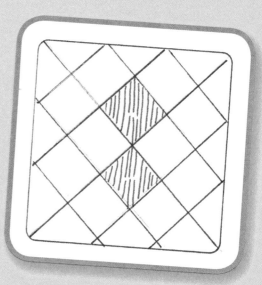

2. Draw vertical lines, using a few "highlights," in every other diamond shape.

3. Draw horizontal lines, again using some highlights, in the diamonds in between.

4. Add some shade for more depth. Repeat this pattern across the grid to fill up the space.

This tangle is all about the shading. Try it and watch your picture come to life.

The following tangles have been used in this project:

YINCUT
Knightsbridge (pp12-13)
Tipple (pp18-19)
Keeko (pp34-35)
Zander (pp40-41)
Cruffle (pp42-43)

This chameleon needs to hide among the leaves. I've used Yincut to give him a helping hand.

61

# Heartrope

Heartrope is a great tangle to use for borders or for running through the middle of your creations. Let's give it a try!

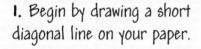

**1.** Begin by drawing a short diagonal line on your paper.

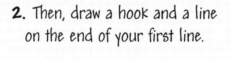

**2.** Then, draw a hook and a line on the end of your first line.

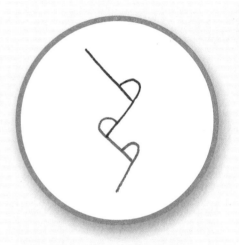

**3.** Continue to add more hooks and lines.

**4.** Add an "aura" around the lines and hooks to create a string of hearts.

**5.** Continue to add as many auras as you like.

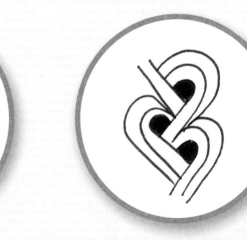

**6.** Finally, shade in the semicircle shapes in the middle of your tangle.

I've used Heartrope along with some other tangles in the picture below. Why don't you try tangling the eagle above?

The following tangles have been used in this project:

HEARTROPE
Crescent Moon (p9)
Florz (p9)
Tipple (pp18-19)
Printemps (pp20-21)
Mooka (pp84-85)

Heartrope can be drawn as a border, in a circle, or straight for lots of different looks!

# Decorations

The holidays are a wonderful time of year! Add an extra bit of magic by making your own decorations to hang around your house.

1. Take a piece of tracing paper and trace over these stencils.
2. Transfer the outlines onto a piece of thick paper and cut them out.
3. Add your strings and draw your tangles.

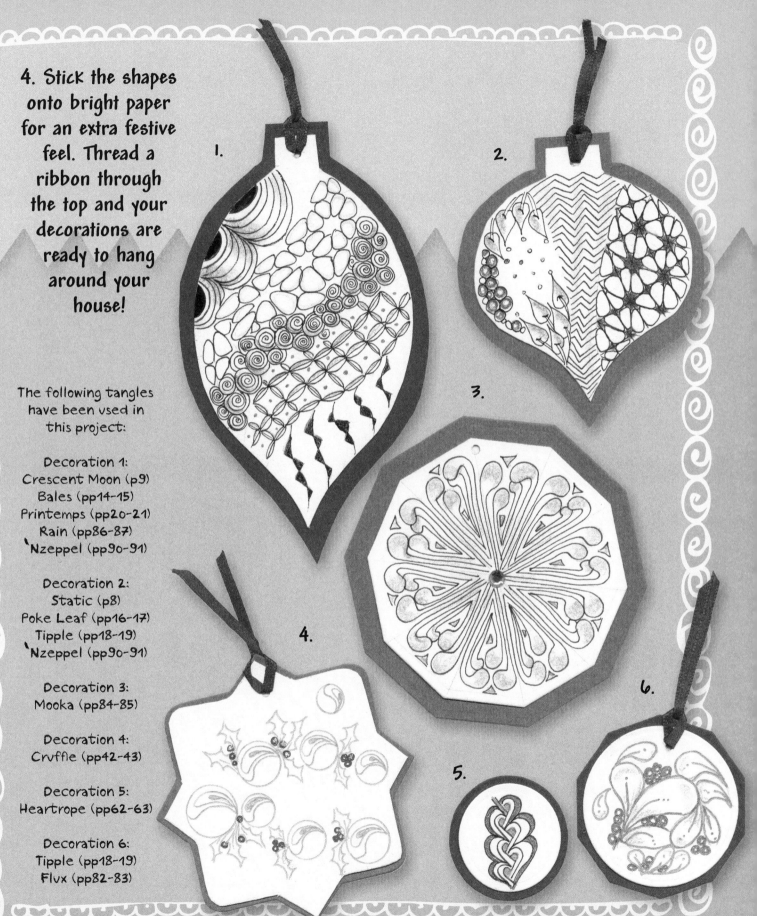

4. Stick the shapes onto bright paper for an extra festive feel. Thread a ribbon through the top and your decorations are ready to hang around your house!

The following tangles have been used in this project:

Decoration 1:
Crescent Moon (p9)
Bales (pp14–15)
Printemps (pp20–21)
Rain (pp86–87)
Nzeppel (pp90–91)

Decoration 2:
Static (p8)
Poke Leaf (pp16–17)
Tipple (pp18–19)
Nzeppel (pp90–91)

Decoration 3:
Mooka (pp84–85)

Decoration 4:
Cruffle (pp42–43)

Decoration 5:
Heartrope (pp62–63)

Decoration 6:
Tipple (pp18–19)
Flux (pp82–83)

# Tanglers' Gallery

Anyone can do it! Look at all these wonderful Zentangle tiles.

Scarlett

Azra

Clara

Aoife

Rhys

Paige

Joel

Georgina

Tangle tiles by children in years 5 and 6 in Miss Randall's class at Slimbridge Primary School, Gloucestershire, UK.

# Finery

Finery is a delicate-looking tangle, so it's perfect for the tail feathers of this magnificent peacock!

1. Draw pairs of wavy lines to form bands. I have drawn three pairs here.

2. Connect these lines with short, wavy diagonal lines.

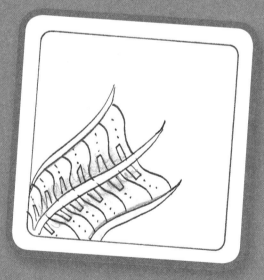

3. Then, add a small rectangle shape and some dots to the spaces between these diagonal lines.

4. Finally, add some shade to create more depth.

You can use Finery and lots of other tangles to decorate your peacock just like this one!

The following tangles have been used in this project:

FINERY
Mooka (pp84-85)

You could add a swirl to the end of your bands for a different look.

# Cubine

Cubine is a great tangle to use when filling large spaces in your art. Remember to take your time with each line you draw.

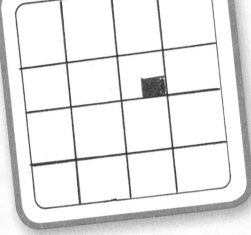

**1.** Begin by creating a grid to fill your space.

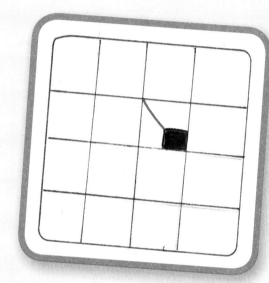

**2.** Next, draw a small square in one corner of each square, with a diagonal line reaching the opposite corner of the square.

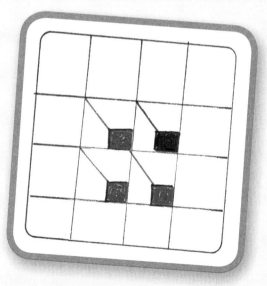

**3.** Continue to fill the large squares on your grid.

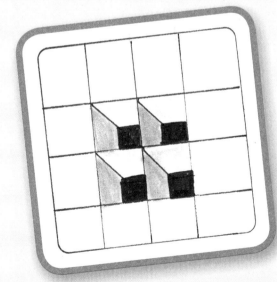

**4.** Add shade to your tangle for depth. Fill in the rest of the grid with this pattern.

Cubine looks great in this castle picture. Its 3-D pattern really makes the castle stand out! Why don't you give it a try?

The following tangles have been used in this project:

CUBINE
Florz (p9)
Knightsbridge (pp12-13)
Poke Leaf (pp16-17)
Flux (pp82-83)
Paradox (pp88-89)

Try changing the size of your grid to create a different look!

# Hibred

Hibred makes a great border pattern around a photo frame or a bookmark. Follow these simple steps to give it a try!

**1.** Draw two pairs of wavy lines from the bottom left-hand corner of your paper, about 0.4 inch (1 cm) apart, to create a "band."

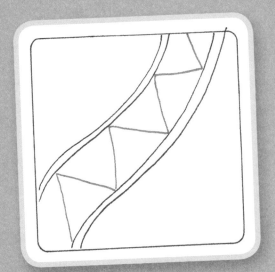

**2.** Add a zigzag pattern through the middle of the band.

**3.** Next, draw zigzag lines around the line you made at step 2. Repeat this pattern to fill the space.

**4.** Don't forget to shade your tangle, too!

Hibred looks a little bit like reptile scales, so it's perfect for the skin of this snake. Can you tangle the snake on the left?

The following tangles have been used in this project:

HIBRED
Crescent Moon (p9)
Tipple (pp18-19)
Cruffle (pp42-43)

This is a tricky tangle to do, so relax and remember to go slowly...

73

# Man-O-Man

This tangle is quite hard to do, so take your time with each line and be patient! It is easier to start with a small space first.

1. Begin by drawing five small squares in the shape of a cross.

2. Add four small triangles in the spaces between the squares. Then start to add squares on top of the square shapes you made in step 1 to form the next layer.

3. Continue to add triangles and squares, following the steps above, to make your tangle bigger.

4. Add some shade to your tangle to finish it off.

Now that you have mastered this tangle, you can use it to fill larger spaces. It'll look even more impressive!

Man-O-Man really stands out when it's complete. Why not use it to create your own giraffe?

The following tangles have been used in this project:

MAN-O-MAN
Crescent Moon (p9)
Tipple (pp18-19)
Printemps (pp20-21)
Hollibaugh (pp26-27)
Barberpole (pp28-29)
Meer (pp76-77)

# Meer

Meer is great fun to draw, and it's simple, too! Follow these easy steps to make your own Meer tangle.

**1.** Draw two pairs of lines across your paper, about 0.4 inch (1 cm) apart, to create two "bands." Then draw a wavy line down the middle.

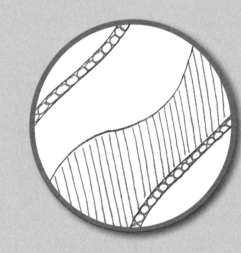

**2.** Draw some small circles inside the borders of your bands. Then draw lots of short diagonal lines on one side of the wavy line, filling the space.

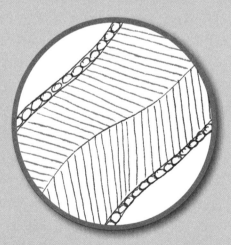

**3.** Next, draw more diagonal lines, going in the opposite direction, on the other side of the wavy line.

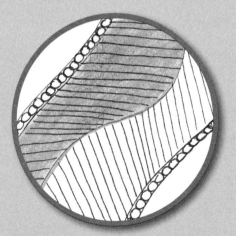

**4.** Add some shade to one side of your band to give your tangle depth.

This tangle is good for filling big and small spaces, which is why I have used it in this cup and saucer picture!

The following tangles have been used in this project:

MEER
Knightsbridge (pp12-13)
Tipple (pp18-19)
Barberpole (pp28-29)
Chillon (pp32-33)
Flux (pp82-83)
Paradox (pp88-89)

Experiment in the spaces between the lines in step 2. Try drawing larger circles for a different look.

# Bunting

Everyone loves bunting! Use it for a great party decoration or simply hang it up in your bedroom. The best part is it's easy to make!

1. Cut out some triangles from white paper.

2. Draw some random strings or more formal lines. It's up to you!

3. Draw a tangle in each space between the strings.

4. Add shade to your tangles to brighten up your bunting.

**5.** Finally, make a hole at the top of each triangle and string your bunting together!

You're ready to hang up your bunting wherever you like!

The following tangles have been used in this project:

1. Static (p8), Crescent Moon (p9), Bales (pp14-15), Tipple (pp18-19), and Hollibaugh (pp26-27).

2. Tipple (pp18-19), Hollibaugh (pp26-27), and some of the squares have been shaded black.

3. Knightsbridge (pp12-13), Tipple (pp18-19), Finery (pp68-69), Hibred (pp72-73), Man-O-Man (pp74-75), Meer (pp76-77), and Flux (pp82-83).

4. Mooka (pp84-85), which I have shaded blue.

1.

2.

3.

4.

# Tangle Time!

Brighten this underwater world with
some marine-themed tangles.

# Flux

Flux creates a flowing, leaf-like pattern, so it is perfect for this tree picture. Just follow these simple steps!

**1.** Draw a small, rounded leaf shape at the bottom of your paper.

**2.** Add another leaf shape; imagine it is growing from a stem.

**3.** Add more leaves, on both sides of the stem. Fill in the gaps between the leaves with Tipple (pp18-19).

**4.** Finally, add some shade to complete your tangle.

You can change the look of Flux by changing the size and shape of the "leaves"!

Expert

The following tangles have been used in this project:

FLUX
Tipple (pp18-19)
Keeko (pp34-35)
Zander (pp40-41)

I've used Flux along with other tangles in the picture above. Why don't you try tangling the tree on the right?

83

# Mooka

This tangle takes time and practice, so be patient and take it slowly. Follow these steps to give it a try!

1. Draw two "stems" that curve inward, following the direction of the arrows.

2. Then, with one continuous stroke, draw two more stems on your paper.

3. You will end up with this delicate tangle.

4. Finally, add some shade to your tangle for more depth.

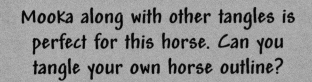

Mooka along with other tangles is perfect for this horse. Can you tangle your own horse outline?

The following tangles have been used in this project:

MOOKA
Tipple (pp18-19)
Printemps (pp20-21)

You can draw Mooka with "stems" that curve outward, too.

85

# Rain

Rain is another great tangle for borders of pictures. By repeating the pattern, it is a useful tangle for filling large spaces, too!

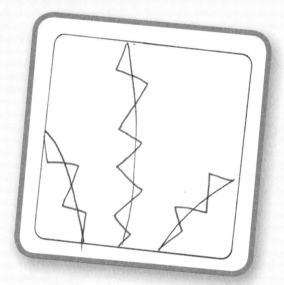

**1.** Begin by drawing some curved lines, starting at the bottom of your paper. I have drawn three here.

**2.** Next, add a zigzag pattern along each line. It can be neat and tidy or an informal zigzag. You decide!

**3.** Shade in the triangle spaces of the zigzag lines.

**4.** Add "auras" around your tangle pattern.

The black shading of Rain really makes the tangle stand out in this umbrella picture!

The following tangles have been used in this project:

RAIN
Paradox
(pp88-89)
'Nzeppel
(pp90-91)

The name of this tangle makes it ideal to use for this umbrella. Why don't you try it?

# Paradox

Paradox is a mind-bending tangle! Its 3-D pattern does take a bit of practice though. Let's give it a try!

1. Begin by drawing a square.

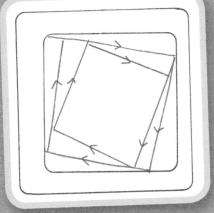

2. Add a line to the top of your square. Turn your paper 90°, then add another line to the top of your square. Turn again and add a line, and again to add a fourth line. You've made a small square inside your first one.

3. Keep adding smaller squares inside one another, turning the paper each time.

4. You'll end up with this busy-looking tangle! Add some shade to finish it off.

5. Try drawing Paradox inside a triangle for a different look.

Paradox is great for creating "animal stripes" in your pictures. It's perfect for this stripy tiger!

The following tangles have been used in this project:

PARADOX
Crescent Moon (p9)
Tipple (pp18-19)
Keeko (pp34-35)
Zander (pp40-41)
Cubine (pp70-71)

Remember to turn, turn, turn!

# 'Nzeppel

'Nzeppel can be a tricky tangle to do, but it looks great once it's complete. Follow these steps to create your own tangle.

**1.** Begin by drawing a basic grid. Keep the lines quite far apart.

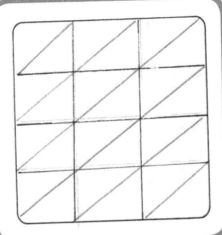

**2.** Next, draw one set of diagonal lines through the cross sections of your grid, like this.

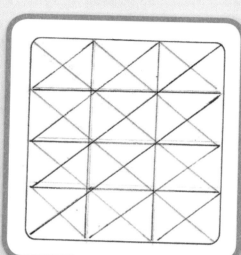

**3.** Then draw another set of diagonal lines from the opposite direction.

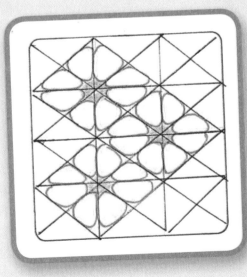

**4.** Draw pebble shapes inside the triangle spaces. The shapes should touch the edges of the triangle, but not the corners.

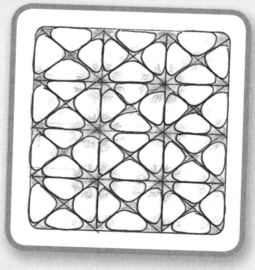

**5.** Keep adding pebble shapes until you have filled the space. Add some shade to finish your tangle.

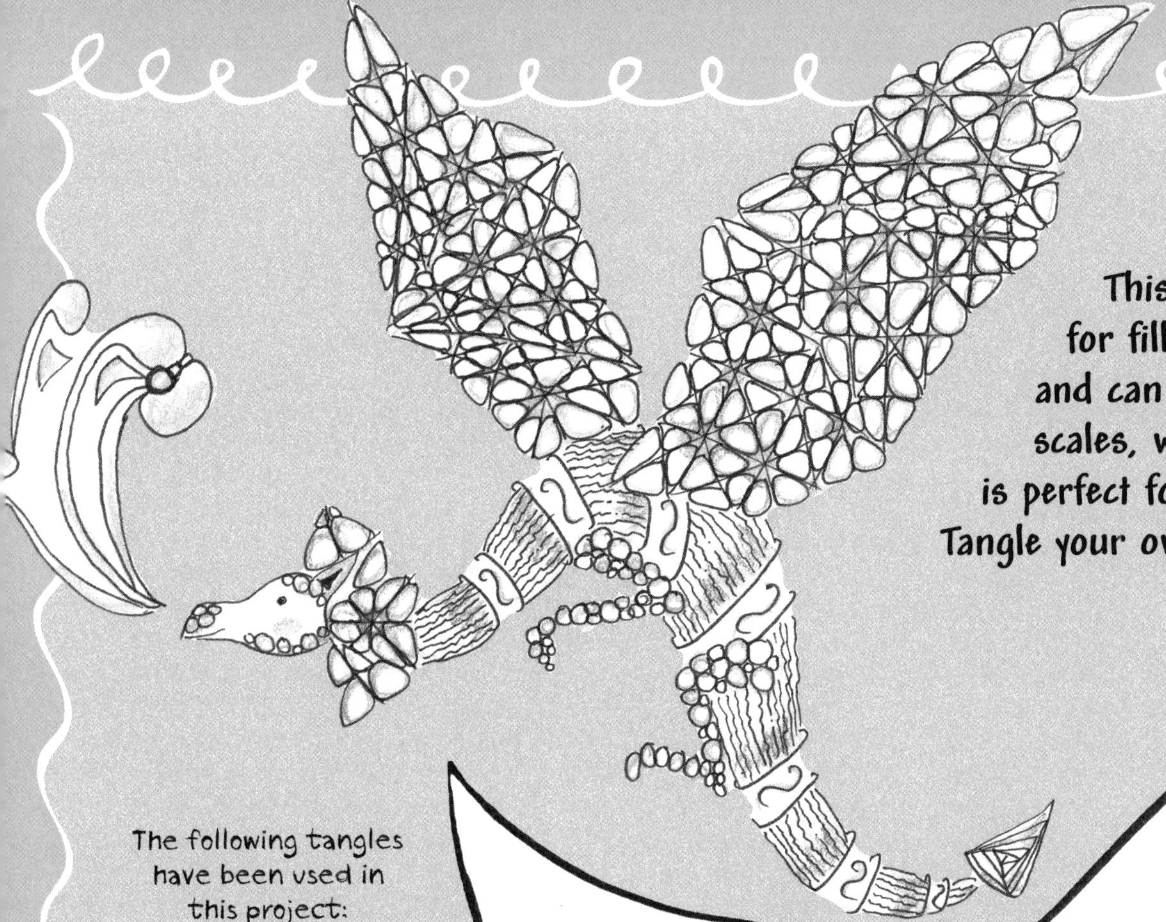

This tangle is great for filling large spaces and can look a little like scales, which is why it is perfect for this dragon. Tangle your own dragon below!

The following tangles have been used in this project:

'NZEPPEL
Tipple (pp18-19)
Zander (pp40-41)
Mooka (pp84-85)
Paradox (pp88-89)

# Book Cover

In no time at all, you will soon have a book full of Zentangle patterns. Why not decorate your notebook cover with tangles, too?

**1.** Get a piece of white paper that is the same size as the notebook you are going to cover.

**2.** Use stencils or rubber stamps to create outlines and a background pattern.

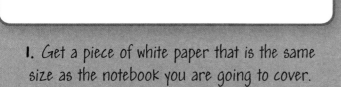

Why not use a letter stencil and tangle your name on the cover?

**3.** Fill your design with tangles. Don't forget to add some shade, too.

**4. Stick your design onto a blank notebook for a very snazzy cover!**

A personalized notebook would make a lovely gift, too!

The following tangles have been used in this project:

Crescent Moon (p9)
Poke Leaf (pp16-17)
Tipple (pp18-19)
Printemps (pp20-21)
Chillon (pp32-33)
Zander (pp40-41)
Cruffle (pp42-43)
Yincut (pp60-61)
Finery (pp68-69)
Cubine (pp70-71)
Meer (pp76-77)
Flux (pp82-83)
Mooka (pp84-85)
Rain (pp86-87)
Paradox (pp88-89)

# Tanglers' Gallery

Anyone can do it! Look at all this wonderful Zentangle Inspired Art.

Plate by
Abigail McInally,
age 16

Man-O-Man
by Lilah Steen Bartholomew,
age 8

Flapper Girl
by Jane Marbaix using
JuJuBeedze (created
by Rosie Hill, CZT)

Leaves by
Rose Smith,
age 93

Little People by Billie Lauder,
CZT

Tree by Emma McInally,
age 15

95

# Framed Quote

Sometimes I like to find a quote and print it in the
middle of some card, then tangle around it.

Anything is
possible,
one stroke
at a time.